Ripley's Believe It or Not!®

Developed and produced by Ripley Publishing Ltd

This edition published and distributed by:
Mason Crest Publishers Inc.
370 Reed Road, Broomall, Pennsylvania 19008
(866) MCP-BOOK (toll free)
www.masoncrest.com

Ripley's Believe It or Not!
Fun and Games
ISBN 978-1-4222-1534-0
Library of Congress Cataloging-in-Publication data is available

Ripley's Believe It or Not!—Complete 16 Title Series
ISBN 978-1-4222-1529-6

PUBLISHER'S NOTE
While every effort has been made to verify the accuracy of the entries in this book,
the Publishers cannot be held responsible for any errors contained in the work.
They would be glad to receive any information from readers.

WARNING
Some of the stunts and activities in this book are undertaken by experts and should not
be attempted by anyone without adequate training and supervision.

Printed in the United States of America

3 1561 00230 5633

Ripley's Believe It or Not!

Fun & Games

RIPLEY PUBLISHING

a Jim Pattison Company

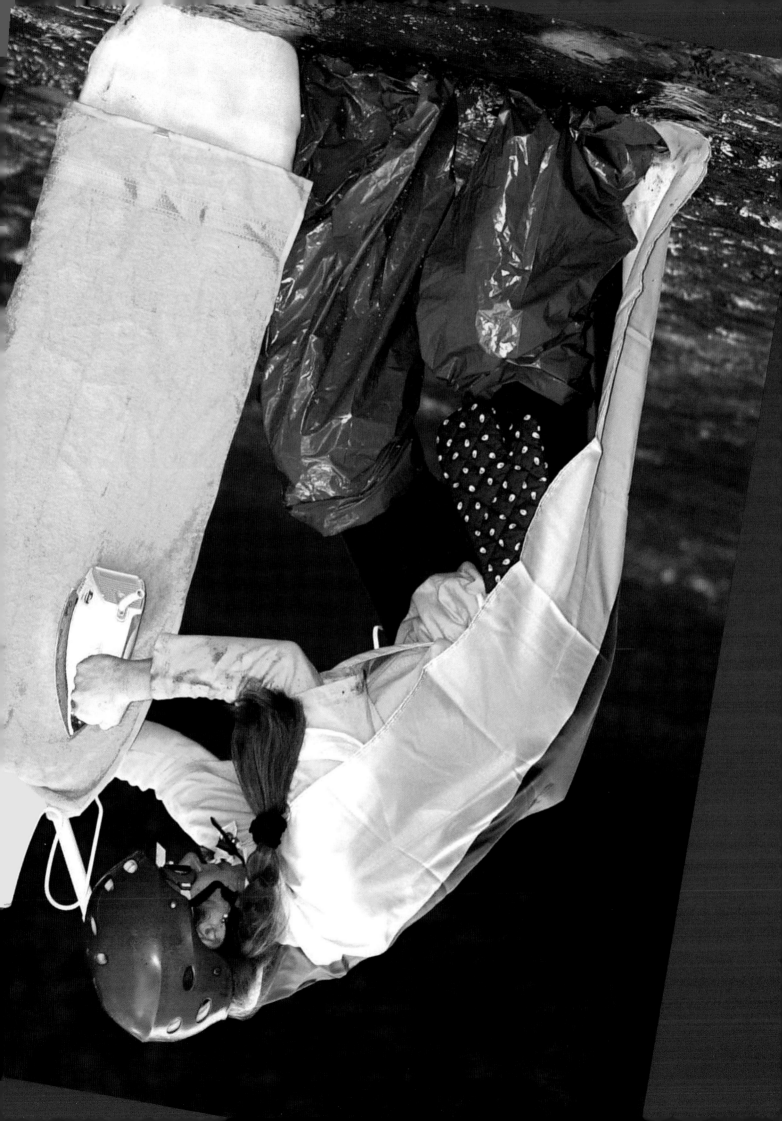

Fun & Games

presents a host of entertaining tales about a selection of jaw-dropping feats, hoards, and competitions. Read about a life-size George Washington cake, a 10,000-piece toy rabbit collection, and the man who pushed a peanut for 7 miles with his nose—all in this remarkable book.

A Russian competitor excels in an extreme ironing competition...

Gnome Man's Land

Twice a week, Ron Broomfield dresses as a garden gnome, complete with the obligatory cap, pipe, and fishing rod, and joins a few hundred of the brightly colored little chaps in his garden!

Unsurprisingly there is no place in this menagerie for a wife. "I'm not married any more," confesses Ron, "but, to be frank, there's no room for a woman. Gnomes have become my life." Ron's hobby has so far cost him more than £20,000 ($28,500), but it's all in a good cause as he uses the gnomes to help raise money for charity.

Sixty-nine-year-old Ron Broomfield shares his home in Alford, Lincolnshire, England, with nearly 1,000 garden gnomes.

People collect all sorts of little men. The fourth annual Michelin collectors' convention was held in July 2003 in Clermont Ferrand, France.

Eyes on the Past

A collection of nearly 2,000 glass eyes was auctioned in 1998 by Sotheby's. The collection contained different colored eyes—from light blue and green, to hazel and brown. Sold separately to adults and children worldwide, the collection dates from mid-19th century England. It is believed that in the 9th century BC Egyptians created artificial eyes by pouring wax or plaster into the orbits of the dead after removing their eyes. A precious stone was inserted into the middle to represent the iris.

Sotheby's auction expert, Catherine Southon, poses with the glass eyes before they were sold at auction.

Bride Wore Green Susan Lane of Toluca Lake, California, creates wedding dresses and bouquets out of recycled trash—including plastic bags, egg cartons, and cotton balls!

Tallest Cake The world's tallest bridal cake was prepared for the wedding of Dutch crown-prince Willem-Alexander to Princess Maxima in February 2002. The top of the cake towered 59 ft (18 m) above the town square in Ommen, the Netherlands.

Harvest Time Otto Wegner of Strasbourg, France, took 15 years to build a clock made entirely of straw—it even had a straw mechanism—and it worked!

Hard to Match A 9-ft (3-m) high model of Cologne Cathedral was built with 2,500,000 matches by Hans Swoboda of Chicago.

Beach Mansion A sandcastle built by M.S. Di Persio of Bradley Beach, New Jersey, measured 8 ft 2in (2.5 m) high and comprised 33 floors, 1,637 windows, 84 doors, and 752 steps!

Thousands of collectors attended a G.I. Joe Collectors' Convention in Washington in 1999, to mark the 35th anniversary of G.I. Joe!

Jacqueline Voisenet has an amazing collection of 647 chamber pots, gathered over a period of 12 years.

GAME ON

- Enough rope has been included in Clue and Cluedo games to encircle the world

- The yo-yo was based on a Filipino fighting weapon

- There are 1,929,770,126,028,800 possible different color combinations on a Rubik's Cube!

- If all the dresses bought for Barbies since her creation in 1959 were laid end to end, they would stretch from London, England, to Sydney, Australia, four times

- Every day more money is printed for Monopoly games than for the U.S. Treasury

Medical Melange

In the Mütter museum you can find such diverse exhibits as a plaster cast of Siamese twins Chang and Eng (plus their attached livers), the cancerous tumor that was surreptitiously removed from the upper jaw of President Grover Cleveland, and a piece of the thorax of John Wilkes Booth, Abraham Lincoln's assassin! Other exhibits include bladder stones removed from U.S. Chief Justice John Marshall, and a giant colon, which is displayed in a glass case. Chevalier Jackson's collection contains objects that had been swallowed and removed as well as 3,000 items retrieved from human bodies, such as a small metal battleship, ammunition, a pair of opera glasses, and dentures. Arguably the oddest attraction, however, is the body of the "Soap Woman." She died of Yellow Fever in the 19th century and was buried in soil containing chemicals that turned her body to soap!

The Mütter Museum in Philadelphia is home to some of the world's strangest displays, such as skulls, a cancerous tumor, and even bladder stones!

Navel Power Graham Barker of Perth, Australia, has been collecting his own navel fluff since 1984. He keeps the 0.5 oz (15.4 g) ball of fluff in his bathroom to show visitors.

Worth One's Salt John Rose of Lebanon, Indiana, has an incredible collection of over 2,000 salt and pepper shakers.

Fencing Master Jesse S. James of Maywood, California, used to be hooked on barbed wire and collected over 200 different types!

Mettle Morris Karelfsky of Tamarac, Florida, has made more than 500 chairs—some only one-sixteenth of an inch thick—out of tin cans.

Matchless James A. Davis of Caryville, Tennessee, constructed a violin made from 5,327 matches. He kept it in a special case built from 18,593 matches.

À la carte Jacques Rouetof of Paris, France, has a collection of over 15,000 menus, including one from the Elysée Palace in 1905, honoring the King and Queen of Spain, listing 29 courses!

READY FOR TURBULENCE
Dutchman Nick Vermeulen is the man to know if you're a queasy traveler. Nick is the proud owner of a growing collection of over 2,000 airline sickbags!

Maybe Tomorrow "Procrastinate Now" is the motto of the Philadelphia-based Procrastinators Club of America. According to the rules, anyone who fills out the membership application form and sends it in promptly can forget about joining!

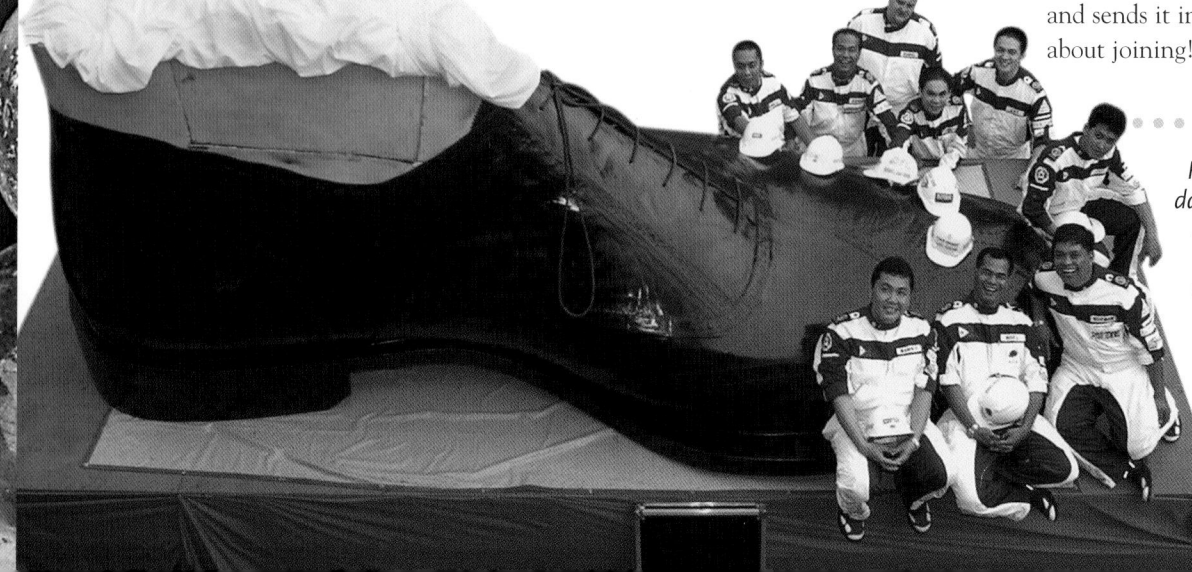

Filipino shoemakers spent 77 days in 2002 making a pair of shoes 18 ft (5.5 m) long and 7 ft (2 m) wide. The shoes, each of which could hold 30 adults, were a French size 753. They were made from 720 sq ft (67 sq m) of leather, 495 lbs (225 kg) of adhesive and 3,300 ft (1,000 m) of thread.

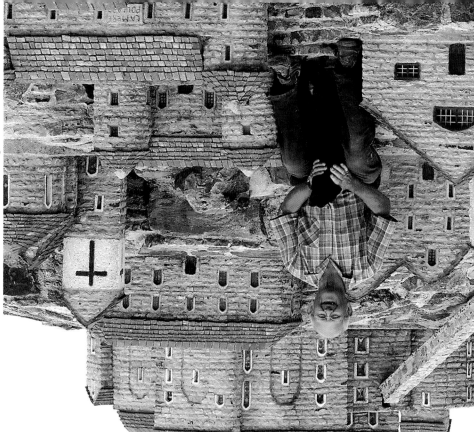

Seventy-one-year-old Henri Chesnais took three years to build a replica of Mont Saint-Michel in his back garden, using 300 tons of stone! He has been creating miniature replicas of different buildings since he retired in 1992.

barely in control of the brush."

Artless Most museums celebrate the best in art: the Museum of Bad Art in Boston, Massachusetts, however, is a shrine to the worst. The collection ranges from "the work of talented artists that have gone awry, to work of exuberant, although crude, execution by artists

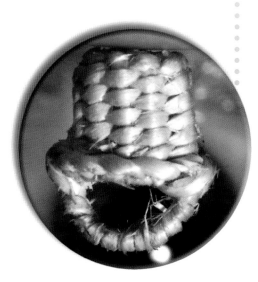

This incredible miniature basket is just 0.28 in (0.7 cm) high!

Overtime Sweden's Lotta Solja has a collection of over 275 parking meters.

Famous Locks John Reznikoff from Stamford, Connecticut, has collected the hair of more than 100 dead celebrities, including John F. Kennedy, Elvis Presley, Abraham Lincoln, and Marilyn Monroe.

Banana Bonanza The Washington Banana Museum at Auburn, Washington, boasts more than 4,000 banana-related artifacts.

Lifting the Lid Barney Smith of Alamo Heights, Texas, founded a museum containing over 600 decorated toilet seats.

Top Dunker Felix Rotter from Germany is the proud owner of a collection of more than 6,000 teabag labels from around the world.

Dirty Bits The Museum of Dirt, in Boston, Massachusetts, houses bottled fluff and stuff from around the world, including genuine dirt from such diverse places as Antarctica and the Clampett's mansion from the television show *The Beverly Hillbillies*.

Jim Jamboree When the Jim Smith Society held its 14th annual convention at Kings Island, Ohio, in 1983, it boasted some 1,200 members—all named Jim Smith. Remarkably, five of them were women!

Upright Citizens In the 1970s in Austria there was a private club for men who wished to be buried standing up.

MACABRE MUSEUM

The Tragedy in U.S. History Museum in St. Augustine, Florida, which closed in 1998, contained many macabre exhibits. Among them was the car in which actress Jayne Mansfield was decapitated in 1967, and the ambulance in which President Kennedy's assassin, Lee Harvey Oswald, was taken to the hospital after being shot by Jack Ruby.

Bunny Mania!

Born under the sign of the rabbit, Akira Tanimura has amassed a collection of over 10,000 rabbit-related items, cuddly toys, and ornaments.

Akira, a Professor at Osaka University, was born in both the Year and the Month of the Rabbit—April 1927. His symbolic birthday may have encouraged his lifelong fascination with rabbits!

Akira Tanimura lives with his 10,000-piece rabbit toy collection at his home in Hyogo, Western Japan.

Nail Biter The Glore Psychiatric Museum, in St. Joseph, Missouri, is dedicated to mental illness. The oddest exhibit is a display of 63 buttons, 453 nails, 9 bolts, 115 hairpins, 42 screws, and 942 various pieces of metal—all of which were found inside a patient at St. Joseph 70 years ago.

Ancient Trappings The Museum of the Mousetrap at Newport, Wales, features around 150 mouse and rat traps. There is a 5,000-year-old device from Ancient Egypt and even a French trap in the shape of a guillotine!

Splinter Group There are more than 700 members of the National Toothpick Holder Collectors' Society in the U.S. Some collections are worth more than $250,000.

Neckwear At Leeds Castle Museum in Kent, England, there is a collection of dog collars spanning four centuries.

The Waltons Deep in Schuyler, Virginia, lies the Walton's Mountain Museum, dedicated to the popular TV series of the 1970s. There are precise replicas of John Boy's bedroom, the family parlor and the general store.

MEMBERS ONLY!

- **Sausage Appreciation Society**
- **Wallpaper History Society**
- **Richard III Appreciation Society**
- **Bus Enthusiasts Society**
- **Flotation Tank Association**

A Piece of Cake!

Pastry chef, Roland Winbeckler, of Kent, Washington State, took a break one day from making wedding cakes in his shop and instead made a life-sized replica of George Washington, standing 6 ft 2 in (1.88 m) tall! Made from completely edible ingredients, the cake was priced at $4,300. Among Winbeckler's other life-sized replica cakes are ones made to look like Marilyn Monroe, Cher, lions, and tigers.

The George Washington cake displayed at the Ripley's museum in Hollywood weighed over 30 lbs (13 kg).

Ripley's
EXHIBIT NO.: 14257
GEORGE WASHINGTON CAKE
MADE FROM SUGAR, FLOUR, SHORTENING, AND BUTTERCREAM

Toothpick Tower Joe King of Stockton, California, built a 24-ft (7-m) high model of the Eiffel Tower from 110,000 toothpicks and 5 gal (19 l) of glue.

Double Drumsticks Over 6,000 stuffed animals were auctioned in 2003 when Walter Potter's Museum of Curiosities came up for sale in England. Among the items offered were a four-legged duck and a two-headed lamb.

Buried Treasures The National Museum of Funeral History in Houston, Texas, is home to one of the biggest collections of coffins in the world. There is an exact replica of Abraham Lincoln's coffin plus the actual hearse that conveyed Princess Grace of Monaco at her 1982 funeral, not to mention a "Funerals of the Famous" gallery recalling the send-offs of celebrities from Charles Lindbergh to Elvis Presley.

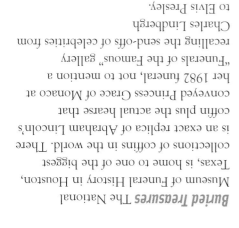

A surprisingly common phobia is a fear of buttons! Yvan-Pierre Deleue obviously doesn't suffer from it as he has amassed a million-strong collection. In 1996 he inherited part of the collection of buttons from his grandmother and has been continuing to collect them since, making his collection the largest in Europe.

Gladys McCrae of St. David, Arizona, made this flag quilt in 1980 using prize ribbons she had won over the years for her homemade jams and preserves, which she entered into state fairs. First prize ribbons are blue, second prize red, and third white. Just a few years after making the first quilt, Gladys had enough prize ribbons to make another one!

Ripley's
RIBBON QUILT
EXHIBIT NO: 13274
MADE ENTIRELY FROM PRIZE RIBBONS
WON AT STATE FAIRS

Token Relic A Roman coin, thought to have been minted around AD 315, was displayed in a museum in Tyneside, England, for several days in 1975, until a nine-year-old girl pointed out that it was in fact a token given away with a soft drink. The "R" on the coin, which the curators thought stood for "Roma," instead represented "Robinsons," a soft drink manufacturer!

Bank Bacon The Piggy Bank Museum in Amsterdam, the Netherlands, exhibits around 12,000 piggy banks, including ones in the shape of the Taj Mahal and Winston Churchill.

Monument to Spice The Mt. Horeb Mustard Museum in Wisconsin is home to more than 3,400 types of mustard. The collection even includes a chocolate-fudge flavor mustard!

Dreadlock Deal A 4-in (10-cm) strand of Bob Marley's hair once sold for $4,500.

Wide-eyed English nurse Florence Nightingale kept a small owl in her pocket—even during the Crimean War.

The Final Word In Atwoodville, Connecticut, it is illegal to play a game of Scrabble while waiting for a politician to speak.

Keen Stroke Arnold Schwarzenegger bought President Kennedy's golf clubs for $772,500 in 1996.

King of the Road Elvis Presley's driver's license sold at auction for $7,400.

Cutting Edge Paul Richter of Leipzig, Germany, has collected over 17,000 razor blades.

Ivan Medevesk displayed his collection of 507 stuffed frogs in Zagreb, Croatia, in 1997. The "Fantasy in the Froggyland" collection, which he bought in 1964, was created by Hungarian Ferenc Mere in the early 20th century.

Tomato Pasting

The Spanish town of Buñol becomes a sea of red mush once a year as 200,000 lbs (90,720 kg) of ripe tomatoes are hurled during a two-hour brawl known as La Tomatina.

A festival-goer wallows in the tomato pulp running though the streets, which is created during the world's biggest tomato fight.

At dawn, windows and doors in the streets are covered in preparation for the onslaught. Large trucks drive up the cobblestone streets and from the back of them, mushy tomatoes are thrown at the waiting crowds. The attack is usually over in about two hours when everyone heads down to the river to participate in communal baths. The festival dates back to 1944 when the town fair was marred by hooligans throwing tomatoes at the procession. At least 20,000 participants from all over the world now turn up for the fruity fun.

FESTIVE FACTS

- **Mashed Potato Wrestling**—July, South Dakota
- **Cherry Pit Spit**—July, Vermont
- **Zucchini Festival**—August, Vermont
- **Most traveled corn dog,** October—Texas

Women of the Balanta tribe in Binar, Portuguese Guinea, take part in an annual festival where they dance while balancing huge baskets on their heads that contain their husband or sweetheart!

SHRINE TO CHOCOLATE

Among the exhibits at the 1893 Chicago World's Colombian Exposition was a 38-ft (11.5-m) high temple, weighing 30,000 lbs (13,608 kg) made entirely of chocolate. The exhibition also featured a statue of a knight on horseback—made out of prunes!

Granny Take a Leap The first Grandmothers' Festival was held in 1992 at Bodo, Norway. Several game grannies took part in a number of activities, the star being 79-year-old Elida Anderson who became the world's oldest bungee-jumper.

Garlic Overkill Gilroy, California, calls itself the garlic capital of the world. Each year it hosts a Garlic Festival, during which it features such delicacies as garlic ice cream and garlic chocolate. It even offers garlic-flavored dog biscuits.

Human Roast The speciality of Chamouni, who billed himself as the "Russian Salamander," was to climb into an oven with a raw leg of mutton—and emerge only after the meat had been thoroughly roasted.

Swinging Couple Aerialists Miguel and Rosa Vazquez were married on a high trapeze platform in December 1983 at a performance of the Ringling Bros. and Barnum & Bailey Circus at Venice, Florida—before carrying on with the show.

Hair Feat Eat your heart out, Marge Simpson! At a 1986 fair in Washington State, Jane Barako from Seattle, using only hair spray, had her hair styled to a height of 3 ft (1 m).

Long Man In the 1920s, Clarence Willard of Painsville, Ohio, performed a 12-minute Vaudeville act in which he added 6 in (15 cm) to his height by stretching the muscles of his knees, hips and throat!

Gentle Giant At Toledo Zoo, Ohio, in 1931 an elephant weighing 13,000 lbs (5,897 kg) sat on a board supported by four ordinary, 14-oz (397-g) glass bottles without breaking them.

Moose Gems An annual Moose Dropping Festival that takes place at Talkeetna, Alaska, features jewelry made from moose droppings!

Diving enthusiasts Mr. and Mrs. Huemer exchange rings during their 1997 underwater wedding in Grosau Lake, Austria.

A devoutly religious man in Kathmandu, Nepal, contorts his body during worship at the Pashupatinath Temple.

Saint of Serpents

The statue of St. Domenico in Cocullo is surrounded with snakes at the beginning of the annual St. Domenico's procession in Cocullo, Italy, on May 1, 2003. Legend has it that snakes were offered to the Angizia goddess as a gesture of goodwill, and that St. Domenico protects people from snake bites and rabid animals.

The statue of St. Domenico is brought out into the churchyard annually, where snake-catchers surround it with reptiles.

Chimp Charm Lucy, a chimp with an Amsterdam circus, was so desperate for a mate in 2001 that she kept jumping from her podium to kiss men in the audience. The circus director remarked: "She prefers fat men. And because she's an adult she has a lot of force in her arms. It's not easy to pull her off men she likes."

Bottled Up Argentine contortionist Hugo Zamaratte can fold his 5 ft 9 in (1.8 m) body into a bottle just 26 in (66 cm) high and 18 in (46 cm) wide.

Loose Lips One of the chief attractions at the 1933 Believe It or Not! Odditorium at the World's Fair in Chicago was Mrs. Margaret Hayes of New York who, as a gurning champion, had perfected the art of swallowing her nose!

Big Mouth Sam Simpson of Avalon, California, could hold three billiard balls or a baseball in his mouth—and whistle at the same time.

Nambla, a clown wearing extreme make-up, including a lit candle placed on his head, enters into the spirit at the Burning Man Festival in the Nevada Desert. Up to 30,000 people travel to this annual arts festival held in the barren desert, where a temporary civilization is created. Participants go to great lengths to create and take art into the desert, set it up and then burn it on the final day of the festival.

Man of Stone Harry J. Overdurff of Dubois, Pennsylvania, was a man who turned to stone. Baffling scientists, his flesh solidified to be as hard as a rock. Unable to move any part of his body except his lips, he could support 800 lbs (363 kg) balanced on his body between his head and knees.

Leg Lock In 2001 during rehearsals a contortionist got one of his legs stuck round his neck for two hours. Kazakhstan-born Birkine was carrying out his daily routine with the Netherlands National Circus when his leg locked as he twisted it behind him. He had to remain on his pedestal until an osteopath arrived. He later lamented: "I think I didn't warm up properly."

Bubble Wrap Richard Faverty of Chicago, Illinois, can blow bubbles large enough to completely enclose his body.

Short Cut During the 1970s, Professor Len Tomlin of England had a traveling flea circus featuring Bonzo, a flea that mowed a tiny lawn with a miniature lawnmower.

Elephant Charged Mary, a circus elephant, charged with killing three men at Erwin, Tennessee, in 1916, was lynched on a steel cable before a crowd of 5,000.

Termites Take Off Every March the 700 members of the American Association of Aardvark Aficionados celebrate National Aardvark Week!

Tongue Tied Habu Koller could lift weights of 105 lbs (48 kg) with his tongue!

REVERSE BEEF

New York prankster Brian G. Hughes (1849–1924) told the press that he was financing an expedition to South America to bring back a little-known creature called a reetsa. When news appeared that one had been captured, thousands of New Yorkers lined the city docks waiting to catch their first glimpse of the elusive beast. The gangplank was positioned—and then an ordinary steer was led down backward off the ship. "Reetsa" is "a steer" spelt backward!

Bare Faced Prank Las Vegas promoter Michael Burdick created an uproar in 2003 when he announced that he was selling $10,000 safaris to men wishing to hunt down naked women in the desert with paintball guns. Women's groups protested until Burdick revealed it was all a hoax.

Sea Monster Thousands of New Yorkers were fooled by a sea serpent constructed by German archaeologist Albert Koch. He unveiled the 114-ft (35-m) long skeleton of what he claimed was an extinct marine reptile at Broadway's Apollo Saloon in 1845. Soon visitors paying 25 cents a head flocked to view the monster, which Koch said he had dug up on an expedition to Alabama. An anatomist, however, exposed the serpent as a fraud, revealing that it was actually a composite of several specimens of an extinct whale called a zeuglodon. A typical zeugolodon measured only 40 ft (12 m) long. Koch had simply joined a few bits and pieces together.

In 1842, as part of an elaborate hoax, the New York Herald astounded the world with an astonishing headline—"Mermaids are Real!" Nearly a century later, in 1939, Robert Ripley displayed a "mermaid" at his New York City Odditorium. There are very few of these hoax mermaids now in existence. Made from the front half of a monkey and the back half of a fish, for several decades they tricked audiences into thinking they were the real thing!

Home of the Whopper On April 1, 1998 Burger King published a full-page advertisement in *USA Today* announcing the introduction of the "Left-Handed Whopper" to its menus, designed to accommodate the 32 million left-handed people in America.

Wasp Sting In 1949 Phil Shone, a radio disc jockey in New Zealand, warned listeners that a mile-wide wasp swarm was heading straight for Auckland. He urged people to combat the threat by wearing their socks over their trousers when leaving for work and by placing honey-smeared traps outside their homes. Hundreds of gullible listeners took his advice.

April Fool On April 1, 1996, the *New York Times* stated that fast food chain Taco Bell was purchasing the Liberty Bell, to be known henceforth as the Taco Liberty Bell. Thousands rang the National Historic Park to protest!

Extreme Flyer

On July 31, 2003, Austrian extreme sports fanatic Felix Baumgartner became the first person to fly unaided across the English Channel.

Thirty-four-year-old Baumgartner, who had previously made history by parachuting from the world's tallest building, Malaysia's Petronas Towers, and from the statue of Christ in Rio de Janeiro, completed the epic crossing to France with a 5.9 ft (1.8 m) carbon fiber wing strapped to his back. Jumping from a plane 30,000 ft (9,000 m) above Dover on the English coast at a temperature of –40°C (–40°F), he relied on his oxygen supply as he began hurtling toward the ground at speeds of up to 225 mph (362 km/h). After gliding for 22 mi (35 km), he opened his parachute and landed on the French coast near Calais. The journey took 14 minutes. Baumgartner said: "It was pretty cold up there, but you don't feel like you are going down more than 27,000 ft [8,230 m]. You feel like you are flying forever. All I thought was, I hope I make it to the other side."

Felix Baumgartner wore only an aerodynamic jumpsuit, a parachute, a carbon-fiber wing, and an oxygen tank as he flew through the air. He had prepared for his flight with three years of rigorous training, which involved strapping himself onto the top of a speeding Porsche.

On July 17, 1999, divers from Bad Neustadt, Bavaria, divided into two teams, and played cards 10 ft (3 m) underwater in a pool!

Dog Bitten in Half

In 2002 Japan's Takeru Kobayashi broke his own record during the 87th annual Nathan's Famous Fourth of July Hot Dog Eating Contest in New York. In the 12 minutes allowed he beat his previous record of 50 by half a hot dog and bun. The runner-up could only manage 26.

In 2003, Kobayashi lost a similar hot dog eating contest to a Kodiak bear on the TV show "Man vs Beast."

Giant Jigsaw Residents of Saint-Lo, France, painstakingly assembled a gigantic jigsaw puzzle in 2002. It measured 50 ft (15 m) by 82.5 ft (25 m) and was made up of 150,000 pieces.

In a Pickle Canadian Pat Donahue in 1978 ate 91 pickled onions in just over one minute.

FLYING BLIND

Mike Newman of England, became the fastest blind driver of a car in the world when his Jaguar XJR averaged 144.7 mph (232.8 km/h) over two runs at an abandoned airfield in 2003. The 42-year-old bank official, who has been blind since he was eight, was guided via a radio link with his stepfather who was traveling in a vehicle four car lengths behind.

Steep Faith Italian mountain guide Tita Piaz once climbed the notorious Winkler Tower—9,000 ft (2,743 m) of sheer rock—with his five-year-old son strapped to his back! Ironically Piaz, who had climbed the Dolomite tower 300 times without mishap, died in 1948 following a fall from a bicycle.

Slug Fest In 1982 Ken Edwards of Cheshire, England, ate 12 live slugs followed by two Brillo pads for dessert—in less than two minutes.

Santa Assembly Over 1,200 Santa Clauses gathered in a German theme park in November 2002. Four hundred and sixty-five Santas had congregated in Switzerland two years previously.

Light at the End In 1906 William "Burro" Schmidt started digging a tunnel through California's El Paso Mountains. He dug 1,872 ft (571 m) through 2,600 tons of rock, completing the task 32 years later.

Out of Earshot Seventy-seven-year-old Bulgarian Kolio Botev claimed a record in 2002 after living for 60 years with a bullet lodged behind his right ear. Since accidentally shooting himself in 1942, he declined all medical offers to remove the bullet for fear that the operation would kill him.

Panting Finish When Jacob Emery of Pembroke, New Hampshire, was given just 12 hours notice to appear at Exeter as a representative in the state legislature, he found he had no pants worthy of the occasion. His resourceful wife devised a plan: she managed to catch a sheep, shear it, card the wool, spin and weave it, in time to produce a pair of pants fit for Emery to wear —all in one night!

Week in Oatmeal In 1988 pub landlord Philip Heard of Hanam, Bristol, England, sat in a bathtub filled with cold porridge for a total time of 122 hr 30 min.

Doorman A carpenter walked from one end of Britain to the other in 2003 — carrying a 40 lbs (18 kg) pine door on his back. Brian Walker took five weeks to complete the 871-mi (1,401-km) trek from Land's End in Cornwall to the Scottish outpost of John o'Groats. He said he was inspired by his father having once carried a door home from a builder's yard 4 mi (6.5 km) away.

Heavy Footed In 1989 Michael Stobart of Loughborough, England, walked 6 mi (10 km) in 24 hours with Dorothy Bowers standing on his feet!

Backwards Record In 1990 Welshman Steve Briers recited the entire lyrics of the Queen album "A Night at the Opera"—backwards. It took him just under 10 minutes.

Maaruf Bitar of Lebanon practices his favorite hobby—underwater cycling off the coast of the Mediterranean city of Sidon.

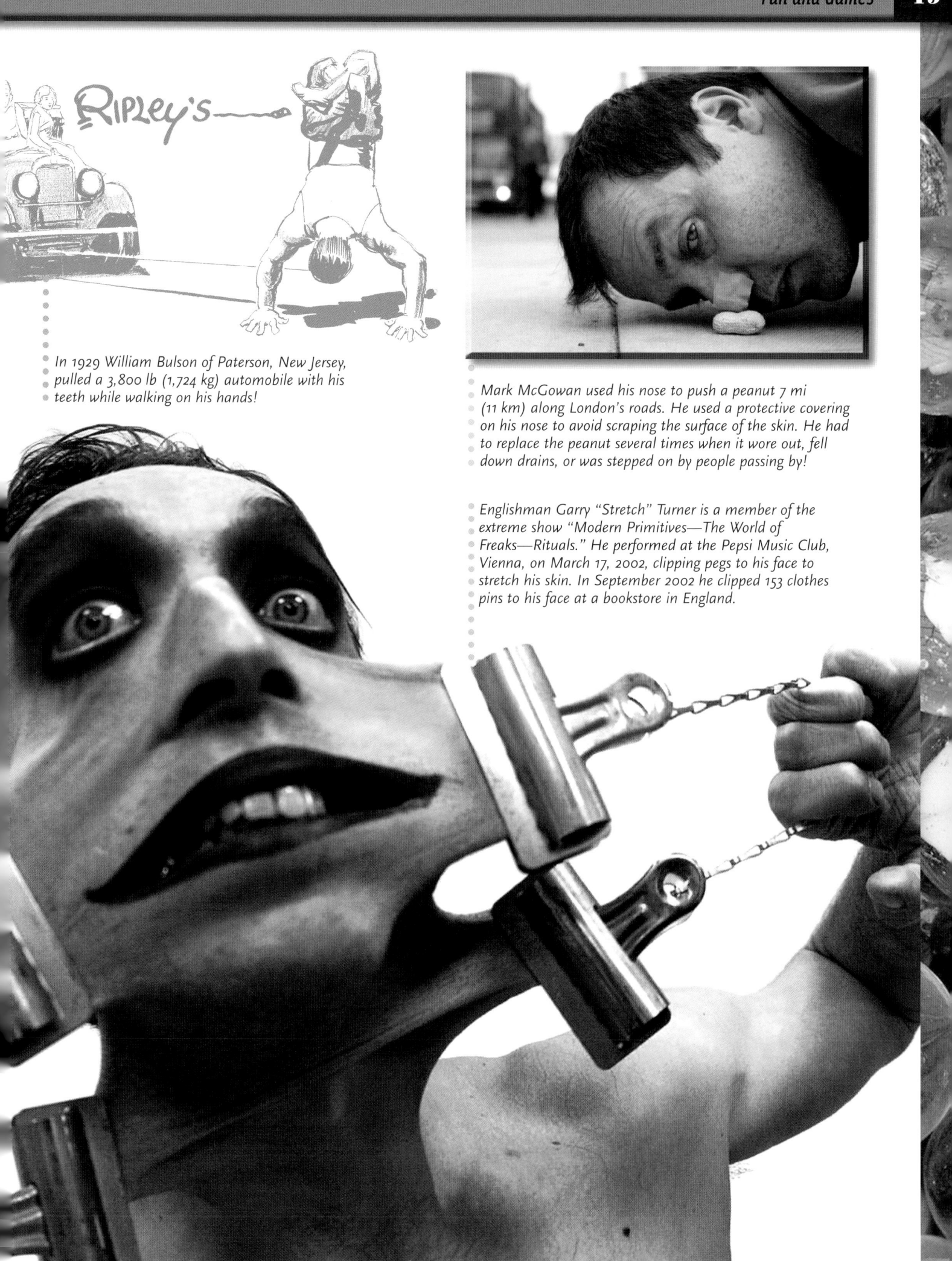

Ripley's

In 1929 William Bulson of Paterson, New Jersey, pulled a 3,800 lb (1,724 kg) automobile with his teeth while walking on his hands!

Mark McGowan used his nose to push a peanut 7 mi (11 km) along London's roads. He used a protective covering on his nose to avoid scraping the surface of the skin. He had to replace the peanut several times when it wore out, fell down drains, or was stepped on by people passing by!

Englishman Garry "Stretch" Turner is a member of the extreme show "Modern Primitives—The World of Freaks—Rituals." He performed at the Pepsi Music Club, Vienna, on March 17, 2002, clipping pegs to his face to stretch his skin. In September 2002 he clipped 153 clothes pins to his face at a bookstore in England.

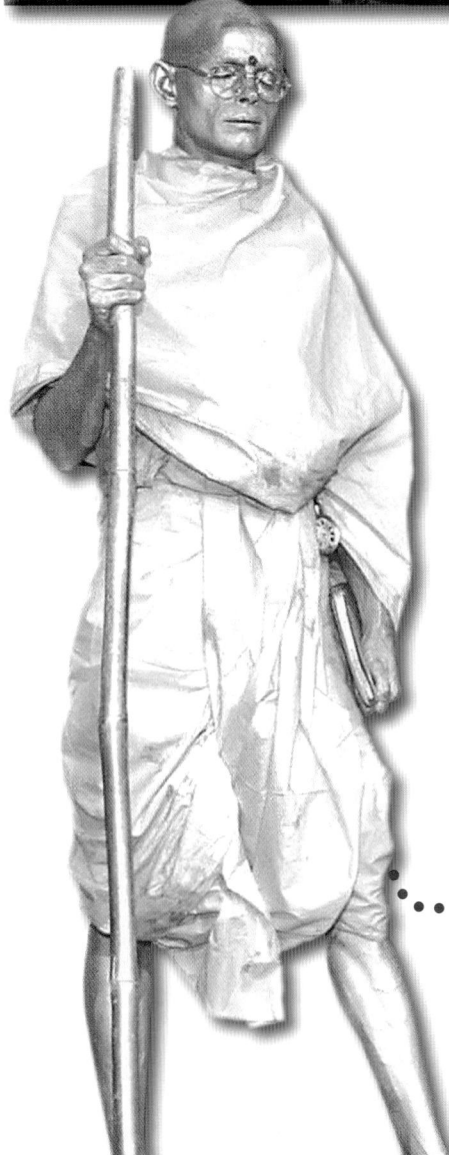

Looking Back It took Peter Rosendahl of Las Vegas, Nevada, 9 hr, 25 min to ride a distance of 46 mi (75 km). It wasn't the distance covered that took him so long, it was the fact that he was riding a unicycle the whole way, backwards!

Italian Job Italians Daniele Sangion and Giorgio Valente pushed a Fiat Uno weighing 1,852 lbs (840 kg) a total distance of 33 mi (52 km) along a 5,216-ft (1,590-m) track near Venice, Italy, on October 18, 1998.

Speedy Sculpting It took just one hour for American John Cassidy to make 367 different balloon sculptures on May 10, 1999 in Philadelphia.

Dressed as Mahatma Gandhi, 31-year-old Akchinthala Sheshu Babu stands motionless in New Delhi on April 6, 2002 for over 40 hours, taking no time out for drinking or visiting the toilet!

In 2003, four Chinese women lived with 2001 snakes in Happy Valley Park—for 153 days! The women even shared beds with the reptiles as part of an endurance challenge.

Heroic Feats A seal in the River Tees, England, swam to the aid of a drowning dog. The brave creature pushed the dog toward some mudflats, saving its life!

GREAT FEATS

- In 1891 Parisian baker Silvain Dornon walked on stilts from Paris to Moscow in 58 days

- Canadian Robin Susteras won a car in a 1992 competition by standing for 96 hours with one hand touching the car

- Canadian strongman Louis Cyr lifted 18 fat men—weighing a total of 4,337 lbs (9,561 kg)—on a plank placed across his back

Pieces of Pi It took Englishman Creighton Carvello 9 hr, 10 min to recite by heart the value of pi to 20,013 places!

Bogged Down

The World Bog Snorkeling Championships take place in Wales. Since the competition began in 1986, eager competitors have flocked to the event from all over the British Isles, as well as the rest of Europe, Australia, and America, to raise money for charity.

The objective is to swim the length of the course as quickly as possible without using conventional swimming strokes. The person to complete the course in the quickest time wins, although none of the competitors smell very good afterwards!

Entrants must swim 60 yds (55 m) with their snorkels through a murky, weed-infested bog.

Bathtime Each July, during the Vancouver Sea Festival, competitors take to the Straits of Georgia in their bathtubs to race across the 43 mi (55 km) course in the Nanaimo to Vancouver bathtub race!

Cutting Up In early May in Japan, teams compete to wreck their competitors' kites. The team members tie broken glass and razor blades to their kites and launch them for a kite shredding competition. The team with the kite that stays in the air the longest wins.

For competitors in the World Bog Snorkeling Championships snorkels, masks, and flippers are essential pieces of equipment. Wet suits are not compulsory, but advisable for swimming through the slime and muddy water!

WACKY RACES

- Lawnmower races take place each year in Sussex, England
- Lobsters race down a saltwater filled track at Aiken, South Carolina
- Once a year, grandfathers and grandsons get together in teams in Fort Worth, Texas, to race curled-up armadillos by rolling them over a flat course
- At the World's Greatest Lizard Race in Lovington, New Mexico, contestants are disqualified if they eat their rivals!

Hot Buns and Iced Cakes

Men and women from 15 countries sweat it out to see who can last the longest at the World Sauna-Sitting Championships in Finland. Every 30 seconds, 1 pt (0.5 l) of water is poured on to the stone oven to raise the temperature. Natalia Trifanova was crowned Sauna Queen. "I'm pink but happy," she said afterward.

Leo Pusa (right) won the contest in 110°C (230°F) of heat, on August 5, 2000, in a time of 12 minutes, 5 seconds! In 2003 Timo Kaukonen won with a time of 16 minutes, 15 seconds.

In 1933 in an ice sitting contest Gus Simmons (left) sat on an ice block for an incredible 27 hours, 10 minutes, but was disqualified because he was running a temperature of 102°F (39°C).

Fishing with Feelings The World Flounder-Tramping Championships were first staged in 1976 to settle a wager as to who could catch the biggest flounder in Scotland's Urr estuary. The flounder, a flatfish, lies on the bottom of the shallow estuary and buries itself in the mud when the tide goes out. Some 200 competitors wade into chest-high water with bare feet, searching for the tell-tale wriggle beneath their toes. The fish can be captured either with a three-pronged spear or by hand. The flounder must be alive at the weigh-in.

Dead Heat Goodwater, Alabama, hosts an annual Casket Race, whereby a live "body" carrying a cup of water is carried by a pallbearer over a winding course. The winner is the pall bearer who spills the least water!

Pudding Bash For 150 years a pub in Lancashire, England, has staged the World Black Pudding Knocking Championships. Competitors travel from as far as Canada, Australia, and the U.S.A. Each competitor gets three throws of a black pudding—a regional sausage made from pigs' blood and fat—to dislodge a series of Yorkshire puddings from a platform 20 ft (6 m) up a wall of the bar.

Fast Flock In 1993 Margaret Davis of County Durham, England, won the first Scottish Sheep Counting Championships by accurately counting 283 animals as they ran by!

As part of the celebrations to mark the 500th anniversary of a town in Belarus, willing participants paid 100 Belarus rubles ($1) for the opportunity to catch as many fish as possible in three minutes with their bare hands!

RUNAWAY CHEESE!

Gloucestershire, England, is home to an annual cheese-rolling contest. As the starter counts to three, 7 lbs (3.2 kg) circular Double Gloucester cheeses are set in motion down a steep hill. At a further count of four, the runners start to chase their cheese! Anyone who manages to catch theirs before it reaches the bottom of the hill, gets to keep it. The prize is worth the effort, but the risk of injury is high!

The World Toe Wrestling Championships are held each year in Derbyshire, England. Opponents sit on the floor facing each other and "wrestle" using only one of their big toes while the other foot is raised off the floor. The first to pin down their opponent wins!

Pun Fun! The O'Henry Pun-Off World Championships, held annually in May in Austin, Texas, sees eager competitors gather to partake in witty word play.

Mower Madness Anyone aged between 16 and 80 who owns a lawnmower that can be modified in order to reach crazy speeds, can head to Glenview, Illinois, to take part in the annual Lawn Mower Drag.

Snow Place to Go Trenary, Michigan, is home each February to the Outhouse Classic—an event in which authentic wood or cardboard outhouses are mounted onto skis and pushed down Main Street.

Worm Turners The inaugural World Worm-Charming Championships took place in Cheshire, England, in 1980. The winner charmed 511 worms out of his 10-ft (3-m) square plot of ground in the allotted half-hour. Worms are coaxed to the surface by vibrating garden forks and other implements in the soil. Water may also be used but competitors must first drink a sample. This rule was created following a number of incidents where water was laced with dishwashing liquid, a stimulant that irritates the worm's skin and drives it "illegally" to the surface.

Frozen Pole Daniel Baraniuk from Gdansk in Poland claimed a new pole-sitting record in November 2002 after spending 196 days and nights on his 8 ft (2.5 m) perch. Baraniuk outlasted nine rivals to win the World Pole-Sitting Championship at Soltau and the first prize of over $20,000 (£11,500). His closest rival had fallen off his pole a month earlier. Baraniuk came down only because spectators started to dwindle with the onset of winter.

In the annual Wife Carrying Competition in Helsinki, Finland, contestants have to carry their wives over a 240-yd (220-m) obstacle course.

Ironing Bored?

Fed-up with the mundane routine of ironing, Phil Shaw of Leicester, England, set about making the chore more interesting. Joined by like-minded people, he sought increasingly hazardous places to erect his board—on a mountainside, in the back of a car, in a canoe, in an underground pothole cavern, underwater, and even on top of a bronze statue!

The result was "extreme ironing," which, in the words of Shaw, "combines the thrill of an extreme sport with the satisfaction of a well-pressed shirt." The first Extreme Ironing World Championships took place in Munich, Germany, in 2002. Eighty competitors from ten countries were judged on the degree of difficulty they could create for themselves in order to iron. They were tested on their ability to cope with five arduous ironing tests on a variety of fabrics and in different environments, ranging from rocky to forest, urban to water. They were judged on their creative ironing skills as well as the creases in the clothing. One ironed while surfboarding on a river, another while hanging upside down from a tree!

PRESSING CASES

- A South African duo won a photographic competition by ironing while suspended from a rope across a mountain gorge
- A British pair set a new altitude record by ironing at 17,800 ft (5,425 m) on Mount Everest
- Australian Robert Fry threw himself off the side of a cliff in the Blue Mountains with an iron, a board, laundry—and a parachute!

Under trying conditions, a Russian woman tries to keep her balance in the cold waters of the Mangfall River, Bavaria, during the Extreme Ironing World Championships.

Throw-Away Phone

Ten thousand people turned up at a park in London, England, in 2003 to take part in the first Cell Phone Olympics—a three-day event covering a range of activities involving cell phones. Competitors had to prove their skill at picture and text messaging, playing a game, and throwing a cell phone as far as possible. The winner was 11-year-old Reece Price from Essex. He sent an 80-character text message in 56 seconds, a picture message in 21 seconds, scored 11,365 points on Tony Hawks Pro Skater 4, and hurled an old cell phone 114 ft (35 m)!

Kissing was included as one of the athletic events in the ancient Olympic Games.

A Touch of Class East Dublin, Georgia, is home to the annual Redneck Games, where contestants test their skills at activities such as bobbing for pig's feet, seed spitting, armpit serenading, and dumpster diving! The winner proudly gets to display a trophy made from an empty, crushed, and mounted Bud Light® beer can!

The Henley-on-Todd Regatta is held in the town of Alice Springs in Australia's Northern Territory in the dry riverbed of the Todd River.

Something to Shout About On National Hollerin' Contest day, Spivey's Corner, North Carolina, comes alive with the noise of shouting and hollering as contestants each raise their voices for four minutes to demonstrate their skills. The contest marks the town's tradition of hollering to neighbors, whereby they would yell to one another when in need of help, or to call in the livestock, and families would holler between houses to let each other know that all was well.

"*teams race along the riverbed in bottomless canoes*"

Sinking Feeling College students from all over the U.S.A. gather once a year in Virginia at the Concrete Canoe Competition hosted by The American Society of Civil Engineers. Students must build a canoe out of concrete that will float and be light enough to be paddled without too much effort.

An Indonesian contestant encourages his racing hermit crab by blowing on it at festivities in Jakarta, while spectators cheer on the crustacean racing.

Porridge from Heaven September in Oatmeal, Texas, features an annual festival that can draw up to 10,000 participants taking part in oatmeal sculpture contests, oatmeal cook-offs, and oatmeal eat-offs! Women over the age of 55 might impress the crowds during the Miss Bag of Oats pageant. But the highlight for the crowd is when it starts to rain oatmeal! Up to 1,000 lbs (454 kg) of the cereal is dropped from an airplane!

TREADING WALKING

Carrying heavy stones to keep them underwater and without the aid of breathing apparatus, the hardy contestants in the underwater walking race in Polynesia must follow a 70 yd (64 m) course, which is marked out on the seabed by wooden pegs. The contestants have to walk the course and are not allowed to swim. Spectators are able to watch from boats, as the shallow waters are very clear.

Do You Come Here Often? Speed dating contests involve hundreds of eager men spending seven minutes impressing women. Women armed with score cards mark "yes" or "no" as the men move from chair to chair in a bid to impress the ladies with their conversation. At the end of the contest, score cards are analyzed and any man who achieved two yes scores gets the opportunity to impress further in a telephone conversation.

Dig It! Angel Fire, New Mexico, is host to the annual World Snow Shovel Race. Contestants enter into one of the three categories. Those participating in the basic production category have to try to control their snow shovels as they ride them down the 1,000 ft (305 m) course at speeds of up to 60 mph (97 km/h). The modified class allows contestants to attach their shovel to all manner of items, such as a bobsleds, luges, or even fireworks. However, in the modified unique class anything goes! Past entries have included an entire living room, a doghouse, and a chicken sandwich all shooting down the slope!

Odors Afoot! For one day in March in Vermont the air is filled with the smell of foul, rotten sneakers! Children from all over the country gather to show off their smelliest pair of sneakers in an attempt to win a $500 savings bond and a year's supply of Odor-Eater™ products if their sneakers smell the worst.

• Around 150 contestants show up in the town of Laufach, Bavaria once a year to take part in the International Alpine Countries Finger Pulling Championships. The object of the contest, which is organized into different classes in all weights, is to drag your opponent across the table.

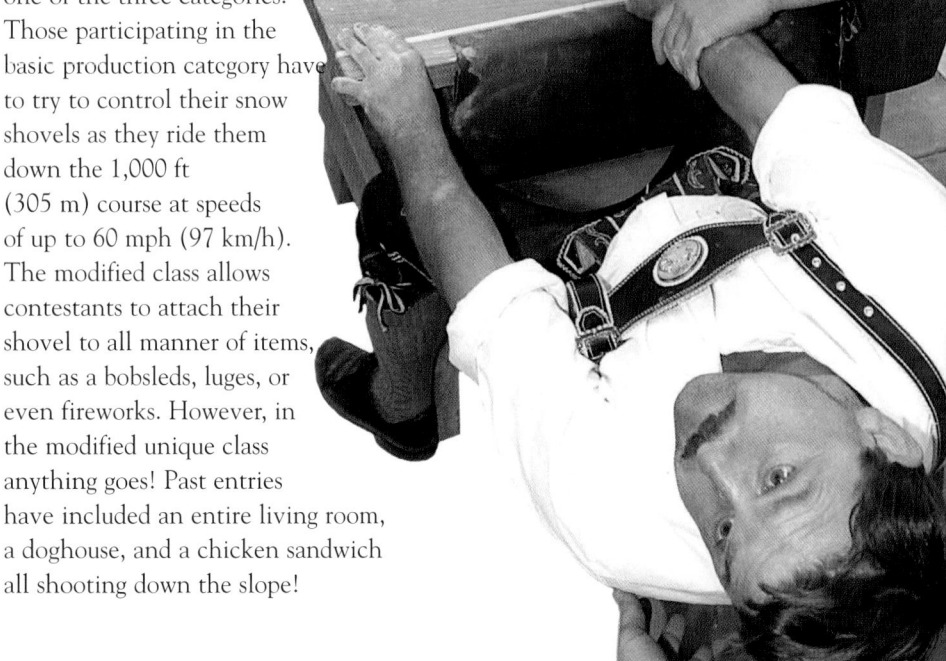

Diver Goes the Distance

At the 2003 Edinburgh marathon, an athlete wearing a 130-lb (59-kg) deep-sea diving suit set a world record for the slowest marathon time ever. Lloyd Scott, a 41-year-old former firefighter from London, crossed the finish line in the Scottish capital six days, four hours, 30 minutes, and 56 seconds after setting off.

The previous year he had taken five days to complete the London and New York marathons in the diving suit, but in Edinburgh he was hampered by an attack of food poisoning. He walked for an average of nine hours a day, covering half a mile every hour, but one day he managed only one mile because of stomach cramps. Not content with his mammoth achievements, Scott then spent two weeks in Loch Ness, Scotland. Using the old-fashioned diving suit for its intended purpose, he waded through 26 mi (42 km) of murky water!

When running future marathons, Scott plans to swap his diving suit for a medieval suit of armor!

HIDDEN TALENTS

- Singer Billy Joel in his youth was a welterweight boxing champion
- Author Edgar Allan Poe was a long jumper
- Singer Johnny Mathis in 1955 was ranked 85th in the world for the high jump
- Fidel Castro was voted Cuba's best schoolboy athlete in 1944. He also had an unsuccessful trial for Washington Senators baseball team
- Sir Arthur Conan Doyle, creator of Sherlock Holmes, played soccer and cricket, and scored 100 runs in his cricket debut

The slowest ever marathon runner, Lloyd Scott crosses the finish line of the 2002 London marathon.

No Frills Flight

Released in Northern France in order to make the journey back to his loft in Liverpool, Engand, Billy, a homing pigeon, took a wrong turn on his first overseas flight and ended up in New York! What should have been a 375-mi (603-km) jaunt across the English Channel, instead became a 3,500-mi (5,632-km) transatlantic marathon. Billy's co-owner John Warren released him from Fougeres in Brittany on June 6, 2003, expecting him to arrive in Merseyside, England, within seven hours. When Billy still hadn't appeared two weeks later, Warren gave the two-year-old bird up for dead, only to receive a phone call saying that he had flown into the Staten Island coop of Joseph Ida. Puzzled by the British markings on the metal rings around the bird's legs, Ida began an exhaustive search of pigeon clubs and eventually tracked down Billy's owners. The battered bird—exhausted and covered in mud—became an overnight celebrity in New York and was rewarded with a flight home courtesy of British Airways.

The winners of the 25th Carrier Pigeon Olympics bask in the glory of winning such awards as "fastest carrier pigeon" and "nicest carrier pigeon."

Lost Balls A staggering 820,000 golf balls are sold worldwide every day.

The Other Cheek Face slapping was once a sport in the U.S.S.R.

Antler Antics Ice skates used 3,000 years ago in Scandinavia were made from reindeer bones.

Fish Wins Olympic freestyle swimmers reach speeds of 5 mph (8 km/h). However, the fastest fish, the sailfish, can swim at 68 mph (109 km/h) over short distances— 13 times faster than a human.

Bowled Over A bowling pin needs to tilt only 7.5 degrees in order to topple.

Bob McCambridge of Vale, Oregon, High School knocked out both himself and his opponent with one blow! Reeling from the punch, his opponent fell into the ropes with such force that the corner post was torn from the ring— and struck McCambridge in the back of the head. Both boys were counted out and the fight was declared a draw.

Known as "soccerhead," this avid soccer fan alters his hair color according to the game he is watching. He even has the hexagons of a soccer ball tattooed onto his head.

Faster Age The average speed of Count de Dion, the winner of the first motor race—the Paris to Rouen Trial of 1894—was 11.66 mph (18.76 km/h). When Gil de Ferran won the 2003 Indianapolis 500, his average speed was 156.29 mph (251.52 km/h).

Who's Counting? A regulation golf ball has 336 dimples.

Croc Shot A golf club in Uganda allows a free drop if a ball comes to rest near a crocodile.

TWELVE-MILE KICK

When a ten-year-old boy playing soccer in the playground of Wilberlee Junior and Infants School, Huddersfield, England, aimed for the goal, he had no idea that his shot would travel an amazing 12 mi (19 km)! The wayward shot soared over the 7-ft (2-m) tall school wall and began rolling down a steep hill. A kindly motorist stopped to retrieve the ball but, attempting to return it with a drop kick, watched in horror as the ball bounced off a wall and into the back of a passing truck. The truck then disappeared into the distance, the driver unaware of his new cargo. Luckily, he discovered the ball at his next stop and, guessing the likely source, returned it to the school 30 minutes later.

Mike Horn took swimming to extremes when he swam 4,350 mi (7,000 km) down the Amazon River in 1998 using only a hydro-speed boat and flippers to aid him.

On a Losing Streak A naked streaker who jumped onto the ice in 2002 during a hockey game between the Calgary Flames and the visiting Boston Bruins was carried off by medics after falling heavily. Wearing only a pair of red socks, the man scaled the glass but slipped when his feet touched the ice and landed on his back with a resounding thud. He was carried off on a stretcher to cheers from the crowd but regained consciousness in time to punch the air in triumph.

Turf Luck Jockey Michael Morrissey once changed horses in the middle of a race! Riding in a steeplechase at Southwell, England, in 1953, he was thrown by his mount but landed in the saddle of another horse.

Crunch Win First prize at the ancient Olympics was a stalk of celery.

Use a Stick! The first ice hockey puck was a frozen cow patty.

German inline skater Juergen Koehler attempts to break his own speed record by holding onto the spoiler of a Porsche that is traveling at 180 mph (290 km/h) while skating.

Barnyard Backers

Sporting teams have many weird and wonderful mascots. They range from simple stuffed toys, such as Millie the spiny anteater, which was the emblem for the 2002 Sydney Olympics, to real live animals, such as roosters and goats!

The French rugby team's mascot Diomede watches a training session.

The U.S. Naval Academy's mascot team wears team colors at a match against the University of Virginia in Maryland.

Touchdown Stroke Oklahoma University halfback E. Cook once swam to a touchdown! When a blocked kick landed in the river behind the goal posts at Island Park, Guthrie, on November 6, 1904, Cook swam the ball back for an ingenious touchdown.

Woodchopper James T. Blackstone of Seattle achieved a bowling score of 299.5 when a pin cracked down the middle and half of it remained standing!

Late Entry The U.S. Olympic team turned up very late for the 1896 Olympics at Athens. They had forgotten that the Greeks still used the Julian calendar, which is 11 days in advance of the Gregorian calendar!

TV Rage U.S. motor racing fan Michael Melo of Boston was so angry that Fox Entertainment showed a Boston Red Sox baseball game instead of a NASCAR race that he bombarded the network with more than half a million e-mails.

Bigfoot 7 ft 3 in (2.5 m) Californian Brad "Big Continent" Millard wears size 23 sneakers—the largest basketball shoes made by Nike®.

Memory Shot Minneapolis basketball star Wilfred Hetzel once shot 92 baskets out of 100 tries using only one hand while blindfolded—and standing on one leg!

Small Target In 1951, as a publicity stunt, Bill Veeck, owner of the struggling St. Louis Browns baseball team, selected a 3ft 7in (1.09 m) dwarf named Eddie Gaedel, to bat against the Detroit Tigers.

American skydiver Jim Suber jumped from the 1,381-ft (421-m) high Kuala Lumpur Tower during the Extreme Skydiving Championship in 2003.

Ten Pin Oldtimer Bowling three times a week, Benjamin Gottlieb of Albuquerque, New Mexico, age 91, was able to maintain an average of between 120 and 125 in two leagues!

Ballpark Figure American baseball fans consume about 26 million hot dogs a year—enough to circle a baseball diamond 36,000 times.

Bloodthirsty! After winning the 1997 women's marathon at the Southeast Asia Games, Ruwiyati of Indonesia revealed that the secret of her success was her drinking blood from the finger of her coach, Alwi Mugiyanto, before her races.

Blunt Boot In a college accident Ben Agajanian lost four toes on his kicking foot but still became one of the greatest football kickers of all time! His football shoes are now in the NFL Hall of Fame.

Permanent Gold A U.S.A. team is the reigning Olympic rugby champions. They beat France in 1924—the last time rugby was featured in the Olympics.

LOSING THE RACE

In 2002 a pair of short-sighted athletes competing in a race around Rotherham, England, got lost for 18 hours after forgetting their glasses. Barry Bedford and Les Huxley ended up making a 20-mi (32-km) detour into the next county because they couldn't read the route map or see the race signposts. With the other 140 runners long in bed asleep, the hapless duo eventually crossed the line at 1.30 a.m.—but only after phoning the race organizers to come and get them!

Slippery Tactics Four players on the Sacramento State University football team in 2002 were accused of spraying their uniforms with non-stick cooking oil before a game against Montana University, in order to make themselves more difficult to tackle. The plan didn't work—Montana won 31–24.

Weighing a staggering 772 lbs (350 kg), world sumo wrestling champion Emanuel Yarborough uses his weight against Czech female wrestler Klara Janu during the Open International Sumo Championships in April 2002.

Wing and a Prayer Playing at the Bay of Quinte Club, Ontario, in 1934, golfer Jack Ackerman could not believe his bad luck when his tee shot came to rest on the rim of the hole. Just as he was cursing his misfortune, however, a butterfly landed on the ball, causing it to drop in for a hole in one.

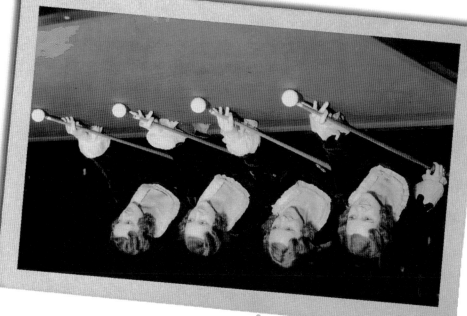

In 1932 the Albee sisters, Connecticut trick-shot artists, played double-team billiards on the Vaudeville circuit in New York and New Jersey.

Half-Blind Winner Harry Greb held the title of world middleweight boxing champion for three years despite being blind in one eye.

Danish golfer Annika Ostberg wraps up well when he competes in the World Ice Golf Championships, which attracts over 20 players from 10 countries.

SHOW OF STRENGTH

Before the introductions to a 1992 fight, American boxer Daniel Caruso psyched himself up by pounding his face with his gloves. Unfortunately he overdid it, broke his own nose, and was declared unfit to box!

Bird Brained John Lambie, manager of the Scottish team Partick Thistle, admitted that he once slapped a player in the face with a dead pigeon! Pigeon fancier Lambie had taken a box of birds into his office after they had died of disease and then hit player Declan Roche with one after he began answering back.

Eight hundred thousand cubic ft (22,000 cubic m) of water was used to build this 50-ft (14-m) high ice rock in Russia on which ice-climbers exercise.

One Good Bite Having placed his false teeth on the shoreline, farmer Millard Carter was taking a drink from Louisiana's Ticklaw River when a huge jackfish leaped up and swallowed his teeth! Carter promptly went home for his rifle, shot the fish, and recovered his dentures.

Ripley's®

MINIATURE POOL TABLE
EXHIBIT NO: 13152
CREATED BY MINIATURIST, HARVEY LIBOWITZ USING JEWELER TOOLS

Pull the Other One Ear-pulling, a sport in which twine is stretched between the ears of two people until one person yells "uncle," is an event at the World Indian–Eskimo Olympics.

Standing Tall At the St. Louis Olympics in 1904, the American gymnast George Eyser won six medals despite the fact that his left leg was made of wood.

No Beef There! Each member of the 1980 Olympic gold medal Zimbabwe women's field hockey team was rewarded with a prize of a live ox!

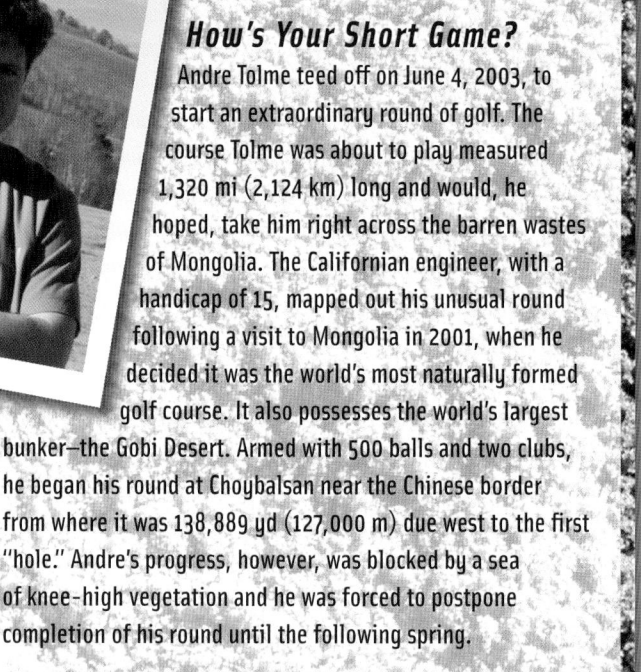

How's Your Short Game?

Andre Tolme teed off on June 4, 2003, to start an extraordinary round of golf. The course Tolme was about to play measured 1,320 mi (2,124 km) long and would, he hoped, take him right across the barren wastes of Mongolia. The Californian engineer, with a handicap of 15, mapped out his unusual round following a visit to Mongolia in 2001, when he decided it was the world's most naturally formed golf course. It also possesses the world's largest bunker—the Gobi Desert. Armed with 500 balls and two clubs, he began his round at Choybalsan near the Chinese border from where it was 138,889 yd (127,000 m) due west to the first "hole." Andre's progress, however, was blocked by a sea of knee-high vegetation and he was forced to postpone completion of his round until the following spring.

Andre Tolme kept on track using a radio receiver and a compass. By August 10, 2003, he had completed nine "holes" in 5,854 shots, losing 352 balls in the process.

Last Try Scottish rugby player Easton Roy marked his retirement from the game in 2003 by scoring a try at the ripe old age of 80. Playing for the Golden Oldies against the Wolfhounds Select, grandfather Roy dived over for the try that earned his side a 5–5 draw.

"sold for his weight in shrimps"

A dead jockey won a race at Belmont Park, New York City, in 1923. Frank Hayes died from heart failure just before his mount Sweet Kiss crossed the finish line.

Shelling Out In 2002 a Norwegian soccer team sold a player for his weight in fresh shrimps! Kenneth Kristensen was weighed before his transfer from the Vindbjart team to the Flekkerøy team, who then paid up in shellfish. A Vindbjart official said: "Kenneth was in top form when he left us in the winter but he has had a relaxed summer eating seafood with Flekkerøy. I think this will be a good deal for us."

Ahdil is a 32-year-old extreme acrobat. His is able to balance precariously on narrow tightropes. He has also walked for 8 hours, 12 minutes on a tightrope suspended 2,200 ft (660 m) above the Tiankeng Canyon floor in China.

Fish Story When Leonard A. Smith of Cucamonga, California, was fishing, he lost his watch overboard only to recover it later inside a fish he caught.

Golf Coast Bob Aube, 17, and Phil Marrone, 18, played golf for 500 mi (800 km), from San Francisco to Los Angeles. It took them 16 days and 1,000 golf balls!

Index

Index

ACKNOWLEDGMENTS

Jacket (b/l) Sipa/Rex Features; (b/r) Neale Haynes/Rex Features

6 (b) Chris George/CORBIS, (c/l)Thierry Zoccolan/AFP/ GETTYIMAGE;
7 (t) AFP/GETTYIMAGE, (c/r) Stephen Jaffe/AFP/GETTYIMAGE, (b) Olivier Morin/AFP/GETTYIMAGE; 8 (t) Richard T. Nowitz/CORBIS, (b) Joel Nito/AFP/GETTYIMAGE; 9 (t/r) Marcus Fuehrer/AFP/GETTYIMAGE, (b/l) Valerie Hache/AFP/GETTYIMAGE; 10 (b) AFP/GETTYIMAGE; 11 (t) Gerard Malie/AFP/GETTYIMAGE; 12 (c/t) AntonioBat/AFP/GETTYIMAGE; 13 (t) J. C. Cardenas/AFP/GETTYIMAGE; 14 (t/r) J. Fesl/AFP/ GETTYIMAGE, (b) Galen Rowell/CORBIS; 15 (t) Paolo Cocco/AFP/GETTYIMAGE, (b) Hector Mata/AFP/GETTYIMAGE; 17 (t) AFP/GETTYIMAGE, (b) Christian Thalheimer/AFP/GETTYIMAGE; 18 (t) Henny Ray/AFP/GETTYIMAGE, (c/r) Mohammed Sarji/AFP/GETTYIMAGE; 19 (t/r) PA Photos, (b) EPA European Press Agency/PA Photos; 20 (b) Raveendran/AFP/GETTYIMAGE, (t) Sipa Press /REX; 21 (b) Courtesy of Chris Pritchard, (t) Courtesy of Chris Pritchard; 22 (t/l) Kimmo M Nytl/AFP/GETTYIMAGE, (b/r) Victor Drachev/AFP/GETTYIMAGE; 23 (t) Gamma/Katz, (b) Tommi Korpihalla/AFP/GETTYIMAGE; 24 (t) Frank Maechler/AFP/GETTYIMAGE; 25 (t/l) Nokia, (b) Patrick Ward/CORBIS; 26 (t) AFP/GETTYIMAGE, (b) Wolf-Dietrich Weissbach/AFP/ GETTYIMAGE; 27 (b) Gerry Penny/AFP/GETTYIMAGE, (t/r) Doug Kanter/AFP/GETTYIMAGE; 28 (t) Michael Kupferschmidt/AFP/GETTYIMAGE, (b/l) Alistair Berg/Katz; 29 (t) AFP/GETTYIMAGE, (b) Herbert Spies/AFP/GETTYIMAGE; 30 (t) Jimin Lai/AFP/ GETTYIMAGE, (b/c) Damien Meyer/AFP/GETTYIMAGE, (b/r) Lowell Georgia/CORBIS; 31 (b/l) Petra Masova/AFP/GETTYIMAGE; 32 (b/l) Anatoly Maltsev/AFP/GETTYIMAGE; 33 (t/l) Courtesy of Andre Tolme, (t/c) Courtesy of Andre Tolme, (b) AFP/GETTYIMAGE

All other photos are from Corel, PhotoDisc, Digital Vision and Ripley's Entertainment Inc.